This Newspaper Editor's Life

A Collection of Columns by Bill Coulter

Digitally Produced by: CONVERPAGE
23 Acorn Street
Scituate, MA 02066

ISBN: 978-0-9825854-3-6
Copyright 2007

As soon as we would get up a few sections of screens, they would totter and fall twisting the braces we had screwed in at the bottoms to weld them together. It was getting dark.

Darkness brings the bugs... all shapes and sizes. We used a portable trouble light with a long extension cord. It would suddenly go out when one kid tripped over it, sprawling. More epithets... nice ones of course.

Then it was on again. More bugs. Mosquitoes bite. Deer flies bite. The kind that made my neighbor's face swell up the other day. Some one tripped over the foundation. Skinned knees. Band-aid. More epithets.

It was midnight. Some of the kids had gone to bed. The rest of us quit. Next day we hit it again. Trouble with the door. It was a sliding door and the track had to be level and installed properly. Down to Grants I went for the third time to study how it was done. By now, Grant's people figured out I was a complete idiot. But they were very patient and understanding with me.

We got the door on and then put the canvas-like roof over it. One of my children remarked how we must remember all these things because the whole thing has to be taken down in the fall and resurrected again next spring. More epithets. "No," they said at Grants, "You only have to take down the roof in the fall."

Finally, it was finished. And so were we. Never to again erect a screen house. But I told my neighbor if he ever bought one to let me know and I would lend him my vast amount of wisdom about how to put one up.

Now that the job is finished, I guess it wasn't that bad after all. It looks pretty good and the family has enjoyed it too. My wife loves it and sits and reads while the bugs buzz around outside. The kids sleep in it overnight and wake up bug free.

Would I put one up again? I'd help my neighbor, but I'd take my kids along too. Without them to help and yell at, and laugh with, our screen house would not be up today.

###################

(This column first appeared in the mid 1960s when we were living on Randall Road in Berlin. Due to so many requests it became the only one in 30 years to be repeated. This was done on July 29, 1978).

Honored by the Church

Few times in anyone's life is a person honored. A few weeks ago, I had the privilege of being honored. It was a very precious moment for me and one which will live in my memory forever.

It happened on a cold Sunday. The date was January 20, 1985. I sat at the head table as senior warden of my parish, the Church of the Good Shepherd on Union Street in Clinton Mass.

My friend Dick Erickson, the junior warden, sat next to me. Our pastor Father Tom Diggs was speaking to the church members at the annual parish meeting which was being held in the basement of the church.

Parish meetings in the Episcopal Church are when new officers, vestrymen (or women) and delegates to convention are elected. Top officers of the parish are the junior and senior wardens. The vestry meets monthly as the policy making body of the parish. Delegates represent the parish at annual conventions of the diocese.

I was resigning as senior warden that day. With our plans to move to Medfield, it seemed a practical thing to do. Bill Tuttle of Sterling had just been elected to take my place. And so for me, it was the end of an era. But oh what an era it was! As Father Diggs spoke, I began reminiscing about my more than 50 years' association as a member of that little church on Union Street.

****

The Church of the Good Shepherd is an Episcopal church. It is in the U.S. Province of the 77 million worldwide Anglican Communion which is a branch of the Holy Catholic Church. For the past half century or more, Good Shepherd has been an integral part of my life. Over these years, I have been associated with a total of ten different priests at Good Shepherd.

The first one I remember was the Rev. Kirby Webster who was rector from 1930 to 1943. Kirby was a swashbuckling young cleric who served both his Lord as priest and the Clinton Fire Department as assistant chief.

George David White served as rector of the parish from 1959 to 1966. His vivacious personality contrasted with that of his predecessor. It was during David's time that the new educational wing and narthex was constructed at the church with a fund-raising campaign goal of $125,000. Most folks said it couldn't be done but the addition and reconstruction was accomplished and is in use to this day. George "Bud" Rogers cancelled his vacation to the Bahamas to serve his parish as chairman of the fund-raising drive.

Father White left us to become rector of the Church of the Holy Spirit in Orleans on Cape Cod where he remains to this day. The following is the lineup of officers while Father White was rector:

Senior Warden Emeritus, Clarence Coulter; Senior Warden, Milton Kennaugh; Junior Warden, Phillips Carlisle; Clerk, William Coulter; Treasurer, James Wiesman and vestry members: Waldo Davis, Dr. Ivan Fraser, William Lueder, Marto Shapasian, Rodney Eaton, Leland Hamilton, John Husted, George Senft, William Lang, George Rogers, Robert Spencer, and Fred Zoll.

The organist and choir mistress was Mrs. Howard Groom, sexton was Elliot "Buddy" Lang, church school supt. Mrs. Ann Breed, Jenny Mayberry was head of the Guild of the Christ Child and Marguerite Johnston headed the Altar Guild.

Mrs. Robert Bursley headed the Acolytes' Guild, Mrs. Groom had charge of the senior choir and Mrs. Connie Lang, the junior choir; Mrs. Harry Birtwell, the Women's Guild; Miss Ruth Maddox, the Good Shepherd Society; Bob Morton, the Young Peoples' Fellowship; Mrs. Bob Spencer, the Couples' Club and Mrs. James Garrity and Sharon Kilcoyne led the Brownie troops.

****

It was during the period from 1967 to 1975 that Dick Knight was rector and the church experienced some changes. The biggest change was the removal of the altar from its traditional place at the end of the chancel to a central position. Those were the years when Good Shepherd under Father Knight threw open its doors to many Clinton and area organizations and served as a meeting place for them on a regular basis.

Jean Hamilton and I organized folk masses which were the waves of the future in those days. We even had guitarists from other denominations lined up in front of the altar, singing their praises to Almighty God in this unique way.

"See this," he pointed to the stick pin in his tie. "That was Ike's pin."

The wedding ceremony went off well.

"Kind of a weeper wasn't it Dad?" my daughter Cathy asked when it was over. I told her how I had some problems along that line too while standing in the chancel. I kept saying to myself: "only girls and little old ladies cry at weddings."

The small gathering of relatives and close friends attended a reception in the Winsor House only a short distance from the church. It is a marvelous old inn, full of the ghosts of sea captains.

My daughter Carolyn toasted my mother with: "Baba, I love you." And my daughter Connie's toast was: "Our grandmother found Art Little before we girls had a chance to."

The Littles were there. They hailed their dad and grandfather. They toasted him because they are as proud of him as we all are. They also toasted my mother's congo squares. These squares are a bit of baking my mother takes great pride in. Sometimes they turned out to be somewhat hard on the teeth. An inside joke with all of us was in telling her sometimes how we use those squares for anchors or paper weights.

****

But the highlight of the day was the wedding ceremony in that little church in Duxbury. There was Barbara and Art and Stephen and my sister Janey standing at the altar rail.

Along came that part of the service known as "the peace" when parishioners greet each other before partaking of the bread and wine of communion.

The four at the altar rail along with the two clergy and I joined in expressing mutual affection. There was much hugging, hand clasping and kissing. The two officiating clergymen were Father Lewis Mills, rector of St. John's Church and the Rev. Robert M. Mitchell, pastor of Art's church in Pawtucket.

Then I assisted the priest in administering the wine. The chalice was given to the church by my mother in memory of my dad. So in that way, my father's presence was represented.

He opens mail. Tons and tons of mail from everyone trying to get their messages into print. Mail comes from religious groups to politicians, from theaters to animal lovers, from environmentalists to industrialists and from bankers to consumers groups. I could go on.

Most mail is from out of town about out-of-town organizations. We throw out about 95 percent of our mail. But we open it all just in case. There is always that remaining five percent that is local or of local interest. This we save and publish.

An editor must participate. He should join organizations; be on committees and serve on councils. This does not mean political organizations. This means community organizations. Because an editor must be tuned in to what makes his community tick. He also must listen. He must have enough patience not only to listen but hear and understand and then take action, if action is needed.

An editor must learn to cooperate with other departments of the newspaper....business, advertising, circulation, composition and pressroom. Because without the wholehearted cooperation of all these important groups, a newspaper flounders like a ship tossed upon stormy seas.

An editor must praise when praise is called for and criticize when it is necessary. The telephone is an extension of his very soul. He must use it constantly, every day and even at home and on weekends.

An editor must be a booster for his circulation areas. That means the hometown folks and the hometown philosophy and economy.

****

An editor must be an educator. This is important...probably one of the most important functions he or she has. It is his job to constantly remind his readers, his advertisers, and his news sources why newspapers exist in the first place and what their role is in the life of the community.

Editors must remind advertisers they cannot expect to place big ads in the paper and then automatically expect special treatments. Treatments like expecting the editor to "forget" to print the story about the advertiser's son when he was in an accident and was drunk or on drugs or while driving, mowed down a dozen trees, or inflicted damage to a building or injured a child at play.

Editors must remind advertisers they cannot tell the editor what and how and when to print news stories and where stories should be placed in the paper. Advertisers should not be made to feel they can dictate such matters just because they are advertisers. Newspapers exist mainly on advertising revenue. Advertising is vital, because without advertising, there would be no newspaper. But the peoples' right to know must never be compromised by an advertiser's dictates.

Editors must educate industrialists. And let them know that newspapers are not mouthpieces for their firm's public relations. They must know that the function of a newspaper is to inform and that's it ....period. Inform. Not to become propaganda outlets for a firm's products or programs.

This goes for businesses and politicians too and for every and any organized entity which may be looking for some free publicity. Let's face it; news isn't information organized to make someone want to buy something from business. That's advertising. Newspapers sell space for it but news is never sold.

This can be a hard lesson for some folks to learn. And it's up to editors to try, in as tactful a way as possible, to educate those people as to what is the newspaper's job.

Ah yes, an editor's job is not all peanuts and pop corn. But I would not want to do anything else. And the more than 25 years I have been editor of this newspaper has brought me a lot of laughter and joy along with the tears and disappointments.

And if I ever arrive at the Parker Milk Company's office on High Street with my hat in hand. And if I knock meekly at their door seeking employment, you will know that my newspapering days are over. And that I have finally let them get the better of me.

But until that day comes, you will know my fascinating, frustrating and delightful job as an editor still has a solid hold as my life's profession.

(This column ran November 21, 1981.)

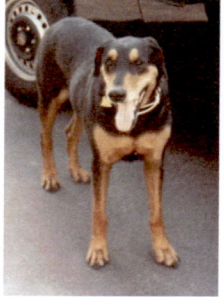

Burning Boat Rescue

I remember it well. It was a hot July afternoon. I was on my way home in my 19-foot runabout powered by a 40-horse outboard. The tide was coming in on the South River that day at Humarock. So it was easy riding. The water was calm save for the usual ripples caused by a tide which moves swiftly on the South River. It was 1970.

I had reached a point just north of the bridge which connects Marshfield on the west with the Humarock section of Scituate on the east. The area is part of the south shore, located on the coast south of Boston. My 13-year-old daughter Carolyn was in the bow preparing to catch our mooring on the opposite side of the bridge.

That's when we heard it. A sickening boom sound just 40 yards from our starboard. Black smoke began oozing from the engine compartment of a 25-foot cabin cruiser. People on board were shouting. Then screaming. They ran about in panic. One small boy jumped into the water.

Fortunately, the burning boat drifted along side of a moored boat in the river. The passengers quickly climbed aboard. Later they were picked up and brought to shore along with the small boy who had plunged in.

By now, the burning craft was drifting slowly towards the bridge. Smoke was pouring from the engine box. And suddenly there appeared on the bow one tiny terrified little boy.

****

Apparently, in the panic following the blast, the little boy had been forgotten. Suddenly the passengers in the moored boat realized this. But it was too late by then. They were stuck in a moored boat. They couldn't move. They yelled "jump, jump" but the boy remained like he was frozen to that bow. He was only six years old.

I watched as the boat drifted closer and closer to the round wooden pilings which supported the bridge. If the boat struck one of them, it would jar the craft so the little boy would be knocked overboard.

Peter's home is only a short distance from Humarock Marine and the scene on the South River of a nightmare which came to life for him some years ago. Peter loves the sea today. He had conquered his fear of cabin cruisers and goes out fishing in the ocean every chance he gets.

Peter and I have a special relationship. It is one possessed by very few people and It is a relationship I treasure very much.

Things are looking up for Peter these days. But he still remembers one terrifying day in his life when he stood fused to the bow on a deck of a burning boat. He still remembers how the sound of the crowd with their cries of "Jump Jump !!!" rang in his ears.

And he still remembers how he clasped the outstretched hand of a stranger who yanked him off that deck: a deck blistering with heat. Some guy who snatched him from the very jaws of a fiery death from a cabin cruiser beached on the banks of the South River in Humarock Mass. thirteen years ago.

###########################

(This *column ran on October 15, 1983*)

And so when I was away from home, I would write letters and address them to my mother...just my mother. She was the letter writer in the family and I thought she cared.

Fact is she did care but so did my dad. One day, many years later, he mentioned it to me. Only once. He said I wrote letters only to mother. Never wrote to him. He never spoke about it to me again.

But it was then I began to fully realize something I had overlooked so carelessly in my youth. Just because he was not as prolific a letter-writer as my mother, what made me think that only my mother cared ? How dumb. How stupid. How foolish.

Many fathers never mention it at all. They are often under the delusion that it wouldn't be manly to mention it. They theorize that real men neither eat quiche nor talk about their feelings. They feel real men don't let on or ever hint about some of their deepest thoughts or private hurts.

I believe we are slowly coming out of the woods on that one. This is thanks to psychology-related literature which abounds. We are now beginning to allow men to cry at a funeral, a wedding, or the loss of the family pet or a good friend and society is beginning to consider it not a thing to cause shame. This is indeed progress.

As I grew older, I began to realize my mother wasn't so perfect after all. That she was human too. But I was convinced she was perfect at one time. Meanwhile, my dad and I grew closer and I realized there was a lot of good in him I had overlooked. How blind I was. Thank God we had some good times together. He died so young. I would have cursed myself many times over if we didn't have those last good years together because I would never have had the opportunity to show my appreciation and love for him.

****

Relations with your children down through the years can be hairy at best sometimes. Someone said they can give you either a lump in your throat or a pain in your neck. Kids today ponder how many children they should have anyway, what with the mounting costs of education and all. The other day Harvard announced its tuition was going up to $14,000 a year.

One group of junior high school students I am with every week as a Sunday school teacher, recently discussed their thoughts about children. The number of kids they wanted ranged from two to ten. People are having babies again. For a time, newly-married couples either didn't want any children or two at the most.

I reached inside the box and pulled out this bundle of fur which weighed about twice its normal weight because it was soaked. The smell was something never to be forgotten. But dripping wet or not, here was a kitten for Cathy at last. She was absolutely thrilled.

Next item on the agenda was what to name her. After some debate, we settled on Tinkerbelle or Tinker for short.

Tinker was a cute kitten. She would prance about playing with scraps of paper we rolled into balls. She would slap her catnip mouse around and chase after rubber balls rolled across the room.

As she grew into womanhood, she became proficient in the skills of the hunt. Many a time she would scratch at the door to be let in and when the door was opened, she would proudly parade into the house with some hapless young bird flopping between clenched teeth. Or maybe a mouse whose droop betrayed the fact it was approaching rigor mortis and who we all knew would never take another bite of cheese again.

All through the years, Tinkerbelle and Cathy were close companions. They would share each others' woes and joys alike. Cathy understands animals and knows just what they are saying and why.

When dogs were introduced into the family. Tinkerbelle would also let it be known that she was there first but she was gracious enough to allow the dog to become a fellow tenant providing the dogs remained mindful of their proper place in the family animals' pecking order.

And the fact is the dogs themselves were usually very accommodating about the whole arrangement and respectfully kept their distance from Tinker in matters of protocol such as who enters the room first if both arrive at the doorstep at the same time and such stuff. Tinker would always drink from the dog's bowl but heaven forbid if the dog tried to lick up a few swallows of milk from her dish.

Tinker led an interesting life. One fall day she disappeared and Cathy spent sleepless nights worrying about her whereabouts. She looked everywhere. She went into the woods and called her name. She searched the attic and the basement and every nook and cranny where she might have gone. No Tinker.

Jim sat down amid a roar of applause. He had laid bare his feelings to the people who work in a firm with which he had been associated for the past quarter century.

One quote from my farewell remarks was: "I say to you that no one, no one on the face of this earth could have a better brother than my brother Jim."

It was a ritual with us that every Friday for the past 25 years, we would lunch together...mostly at the Old Timer Restaurant right across the street. We would go to other places too but the "O.T." was convenient and the McNallys have always been good neighbors and fast friends.

On those Fridays we got the chance to sit down together without benefit of ringing telephones and other interruptions, to discuss the future of our business, analyze the past week's events and talk about other related issues.

Jim was always the business man. The practical one. The analyzer. The worrier. My role was in the news room as editor.

Jim's constant hand on the financial rudder steered the Item around financial shoals and economic reefs. He was a business partner and he was a brother. That's nothing new. Many of us have business partners and brothers. But he was more than all of these things.

Jim is my friend. Someone I can confide in. Someone who listens. Someone who cares. That's not too shabby for a brother. Our dad used to say we make a good team.

Last night Jim packed the last of his things in his office by the front door. Monday he will begin his new duties in Worcester.

He carefully sealed up the boxes. He took down the picture I gave him which reminds him of his lobstering days when he was younger. He packed the painting his wife Pat did for him of the bluffs of his beloved Manomet.

Then he paused to look around. Every thing was packed. So last of all, he turned off the lights. It was for him, the last time.

##########################

(This column ran Saturday, Sept. 20, 1986)

* * * 80 * * *

The Mystery of Music

I can recall so well when I was a pup, trotting down Clinton's Cedar Street once a week, rain or shine, to the late Ethel Greenwood's house at Cedar and Water streets for my piano lessons.

Miss Greenwood was a saint. She had a lot of patience with me. And besides, her mother fed me home made doughnuts that helped make the whole thing more pleasant. For five years I made that trip to Miss Greenwood's house. How could you miss that house? It was the only orange-painted house in all of Worcester County. First thing the new owners did when she moved out was paint it another color. It's a grey color today.

Miss Greenwood shared with me the inside stories of such musical greats as Bach, Beethoven, Mozart, Hayden, Brahms and others of the same ilk. She taught me how to hold my hands on the keyboard. She inspired me when she played difficult pieces for me. Pieces I figured I could never, ever learn myself.

****

When I was a pup, most boys didn't play the piano. They played things like football and baseball. They played war cards at school and swapped baseball cards at home. But no one played the piano or the trumpet. Or the saxophone for that matter. Music was for sissies.

I played football with my neighborhood team. But I missed many a practice and a few games too because it was time to practice my piano. I was good at war cards and swapping baseball cards as long as it didn't interfere with my piano lessons.

Some of my friends began taking music lessons. But most of them fell upon the wayside and many for good reason. I suppose they were just not musically inclined. Not their fault.

How many times today when I play the piano do I hear the lament: "Oh, if I only had kept up my lessons." But music, although it can be appreciated by many, cannot be played by everyone. Those who are gifted with a sense of rhythm and melody should stay with their lessons and remember: it's never too late to start.

****

After five years with Miss Greenwood, I was getting nowhere. Sure I had a deep appreciation for classical music. Yes, I had a fairly good knowledge of the piano keyboard. I knew the difference between the key of G and the key of C. I had learned a lot and I owe it all to her and her patience with me.

* * * 85 * * * .

Lunch gets harder with the years. There was a time when she would ask about her grandchildren and even great grandchildren (she has 25 and seven respectively).

There was a time when we would chat about family news. She would eat her favorite seafood salad sandwich and cole slaw and lots of rolls. Hot fudge sundae for dessert. Another favorite.

****

It's not the same today. As the effects of the strokes worsen, combined with increasing dosages of old fashioned "senility," it's not the same. Now she barely eats at all. She will glance absently out the window and softly talk to no one while making crazy creases in her napkin.

Sometimes she will cast her eyes around the room hoping to find a familiar face. When she finds one belonging to someone she knows or thinks she knows, she will smile. Then she wants to go over and hug the lady to death. Sometimes they come over and hug my mother so she doesn't have to get up. Getting up is getting harder. She will be 91 December 13.

But she hardly eats a thing nowadays. Maybe a half a bowl of soup and a few rolls. She loves those rolls and cole slaw. I show her the same family pictures from my wallet over and over. But each time they are new to her.

If I mention one of my children, she doesn't know whom I'm talking about. Looking at a picture she might remember a face if she is having a good day. And then she might not. Sometimes, she will look at me and smile and say "I love you." And once in awhile she might say: "I'm so happy" and hold my hand. It's the only time she makes a complete sentence.

****

There is a story in this month's Reader's Digest entitled "That other Woman in my Life" written by a son about his relationship with his aging mother who, of course, is the "other woman."

He takes her to lunch and reads the menu for her. His mother tells him: "I used to be the menu-reader when you were little." Her son wrote: "I understand what she was saying.... from care giver to cared-for, from cared-for to care giver. Our relationship had become full circle."

Printed by Libri Plureos GmbH in Hamburg, Germany